CaCO3

To Raphael. Never stop asking
questions. – C.D.

To my beloved frog, Y. – Y.Y.

Brimming with creative inspiration, how-to
projects, and useful information to enrich your
everyday life, quarto.com is a favorite destination
for those pursuing their interests and passions.

Built by Animals © 2022 Quarto Publishing plc.
Text © 2022 Christiane Dorion
Illustrations © 2022 Yeji Yun

First Published in 2022 by Wide Eyed Editions, an imprint of The Quarto Group.
The Old Brewery, 6 Blundell Street, London N7 9BH, United Kingdom.
T (0)20 7700 6700 F (0)20 7700 8066 **www.Quarto.com**

A catalogue record for this book is available from the British Library.

ISBN 978-0-7112-6568-4

The illustrations were created digitally.
Set in Caffeine, Pacifico and Museo

Published by Georgia Amson-Bradshaw
Designed by Myrto Dimitrakoulia
Edited by Hattie Grylls
Production by Dawn Cameron

Manufactured in Guangdong, China TT012022

9 8 7 6 5 4 3 2 1

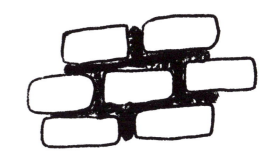

Christiane Dorion • Yeji Yun

BUILT by ANIMALS

MEET THE CREATURES WHO INSPIRE OUR HOMES AND CITIES

WIDE EYED EDITIONS

CONTENTS

SHAPES

ENERGY

WATER

DEAR READER,

How does an army of ants move tons of soil without a digger? How do honey bees work together to build a hive? And how do we, busy beavers, fell trees to build dams without giant machines?

In this book, you will meet some of the best architects, designers and builders of the animal (and plant!) world. Although we have a limited toolbox, we certainly know how to construct amazing structures, produce super-strong materials and find clever ways of keeping warm or cool. We do all this with very little energy and we don't waste anything. It's not surprising that humans are turning to us to help them create better designs, shapes and materials for their own buildings and homes.

To be fair, we've been around for millions of years so we've had plenty of time to test our building techniques and materials. Thank you to all my fellow animals for sharing their talents!

Yours sincerely,

Beaver

··· *Honey bee* ···
MASTER OF GEOMETRY

I am a busy worker bee. So much to do and so little time! Each one of us has an important job to do in our huge colony. As an older bee, mine is to find food. I buzz from flower to flower to collect sweet nectar and dusty pollen to feed us all. Back at the hive, young worker bees turn nectar into honey and store it away for the winter months. They also tend to our queen, look after her young, clean the hive and guard it against intruders. In a bee's world, it's all work, work, work!

WHO'S WHO?

QUEEN

DRONES

WORKERS

This is the splendid hive we build for our queen to lay her eggs in. It also shelters the drones who mate with the queen. The hive is our home and food larder. To build it, we make our own materials. With special glands, we produce wax, chew it until soft and shape it into a perfect honeycomb.

Since ancient times humans have enjoyed the scrumptious honey we make. Now they are dazzled by our smart building skills. We might have a brain the size of a sesame seed but we certainly know how to build the perfect home for thousands of busy bees. Our secret is the hexagon, a shape with six equal sides. It's compact, light and strong and it gives us the most space using as little precious wax as possible.

HONEY

TEAM WORK

OR NOT TO BEE

TO BEE

HEXAGON POWER

The structure of our hive is creating a real buzz with human builders. They are copying our pattern to make new construction materials that need to be light but strong. Buildings designed with hexagons are also popping up around the world. This huge dome made of clear panels and steel was built by humans as a giant greenhouse. Like a beehive, it's very strong but uses minimum materials. Clever, isn't it?

Must buzz off! So much to do and so little time!

EDEN PROJECT, UK

··· *Coral polyp* ···
MARINE BUILDER

I may resemble a dazzling plant or a strange-looking rock but I'm actually a tiny animal, and very much alive! I'm a coral polyp and I live in shallow tropical seas where there's plenty of light and the water is warm. Unlike other animals, I am stuck in one place but that's okay. With my stinging tentacles, I can catch food drifting by and sweep it into my mouth. I'm connected to thousands of other polyps in a massive colony.

CORAL'S TALES

I protect my jelly-like body by building a hard outer skeleton, extracting minerals from seawater to make limestone. Very slowly, over hundreds of years, the hard cases all the polyps build gradually stack up to form a beautiful reef. The reef is our home and it also provides food and shelter for many kinds of fish and other creatures. It's like a bustling city under the sea.

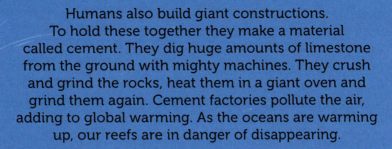

Humans also build giant constructions. To hold these together they make a material called cement. They dig huge amounts of limestone from the ground with mighty machines. They crush and grind the rocks, heat them in a giant oven and grind them again. Cement factories pollute the air, adding to global warming. As the oceans are warming up, our reefs are in danger of disappearing.

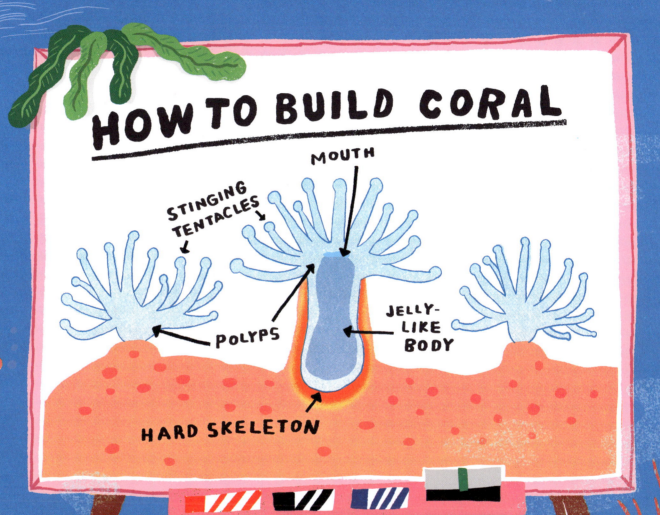

HOW TO BUILD CORAL

MOUTH

STINGING TENTACLES

JELLY-LIKE BODY

POLYPS

HARD SKELETON

Some clever humans have turned to us for a solution. Inspired by the way we construct our reefs, they have created a new type of cement by capturing polluting gases (CO_2) from a power plant and mixing it with seawater.

It's much better for the planet and for our reefs too!

CORAL CONSTRUCTION

Global Warming

NO to PLASTIC

··· Ant ···
UNDERGROUND ARCHITECT

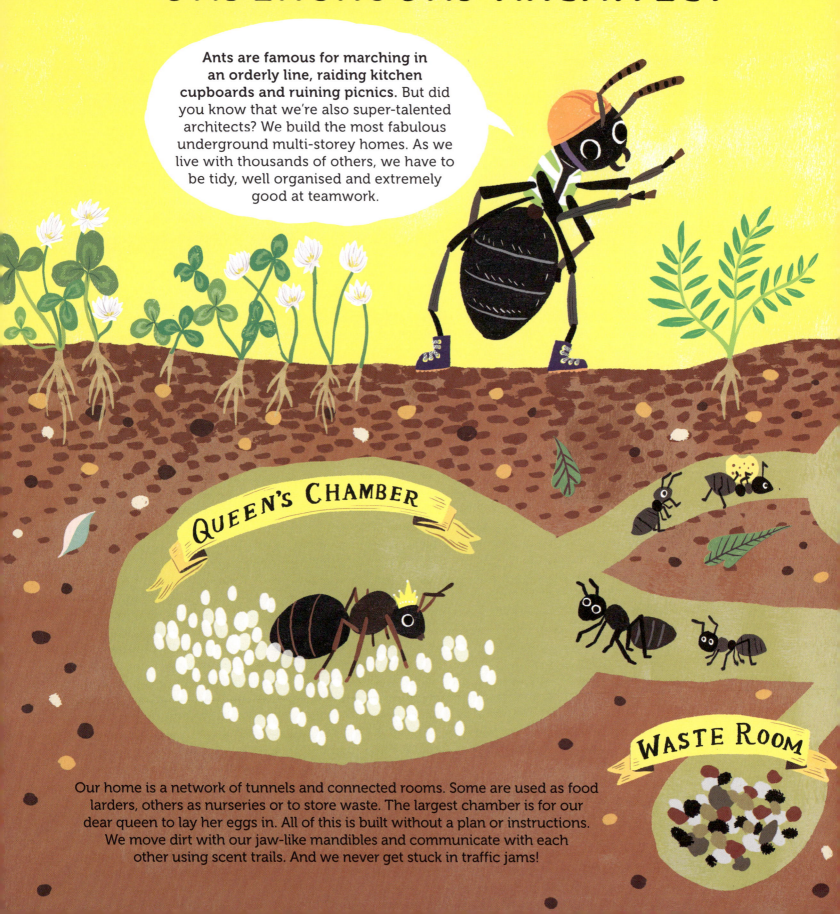

Ants are famous for marching in an orderly line, raiding kitchen cupboards and ruining picnics. But did you know that we're also super-talented architects? We build the most fabulous underground multi-storey homes. As we live with thousands of others, we have to be tidy, well organised and extremely good at teamwork.

QUEEN'S CHAMBER

WASTE ROOM

Our home is a network of tunnels and connected rooms. Some are used as food larders, others as nurseries or to store waste. The largest chamber is for our dear queen to lay her eggs in. All of this is built without a plan or instructions. We move dirt with our jaw-like mandibles and communicate with each other using scent trails. And we never get stuck in traffic jams!

Humans are in awe of how we can design such impressive underground cities. Inspired by our teamwork, they have created instructions for their super-smart computers to make large numbers of robots and other machines connect with each other and work together more efficiently.

We may be teeny-tiny but when we join together we become a superpower!

NURSERY

FOOD LARDER

ONE ANT CANNOT BUILD A COLONY

CONSTRUCTION WORK IN PROGRESS

WORKER ANTS' DEN

15

··· Beaver ···
DAM ENGINEER

I am a hard-working beaver, and an expert at building dams in rivers and streams. I have the perfect toolkit for the job: chisel-like teeth, waterproof fur, large webbed feet and a wide flat tail which serves as a rudder. No crane or chainsaw required!

DAM

POND

Making our home is a family affair and even our young ones
have to chip in. We cut down trees with our sharp teeth and gather sticks
and mud to construct a dam. It slows the flow of the river and creates a
pool of water where we build our lodge. We then add the finishing touch
– secret underwater entrances so we can come and go as we please.
The new pool also provides a home and food to ducks,
fish, insects and many other animals.

RIVER LODGE

UNDERWATER ENTRANCE

BEAVER BUILDING SITE

Our engineering work could be good for humans too! With climate change
bringing more floods and droughts, we can help by slowing down the flow of rivers
and storing water when it rains a lot. A natural beaver solution to flood defence!
We just need a bit of space to get on with our building work.

Can't stay, must beaver away!

··· Gopher tortoise ···
BURROW SHARING

I might be a slow and ancient reptile but I am also a hugely experienced builder. My home is the southeast of the United States, where I dig deep burrows to shelter from the sun, the cold and frequent wildfires. My burrow is simple and efficient. It's a very long tunnel, with one entrance and wide enough for me to turn around.

Dry, sandy soil is perfect for deep excavation. I use my large shovel-like front legs to dig, whilst my strong hind legs give me serious pushing power. My home is comfy and it never gets too hot, too cold, too damp or too dry.

GOPHER TORTOISE'S BURROW →

I don't share my abode with other tortoises but I have many guests. Once I have dug my burrow, lots of other animals move in, from frogs and mice, to scorpions and snakes. Being a vegetarian, I am no threat to any of them and my hard shell protects me from anyone tempted by a tasty tortoise snack.

Few creatures around here have my digging ability. If it weren't for me, many would be in real trouble. Perhaps humans can learn from an old gopher tortoise how to build their homes and cities to help other animals to thrive. **We can all co-exist happily together!**

19

HOME DESIGNS

Animal architects like us build for different reasons: to make a home for our young, to stay warm or cool, for somewhere to snooze or even to show off. Our constructions are made with materials we can easily get our hands, paws or claws on. Everything is locally sourced and waste free – apart from anything we borrow from humans!

Chimpanzee
A BED WITH A VIEW

I build for a good night's sleep! Every day I make a new nest for the perfect place to sleep that night. I choose the best tree and weave its bendy branches together into a sturdy platform. I add a soft mattress of fresh leaves for comfort and snuggle up. With my engineering skills, there is no risk of falling out!

Caddisfly larva
A HOUSE OF STONES

I build to protect myself! When I grow up, I will fly away. But as a small larva, I am vulnerable in my underwater world. So I build a mobile home by gathering pebbles, sand and twigs and gluing them together with a self-made sticky silk. Everywhere I go, my home goes too!

Satin bowerbird
GRAND DESIGN

I build to impress a mate! My construction starts with two walls of sticks and a passage in the middle. I then create an impressive display of brightly coloured treasures – petals, feathers, shells, berries or even things borrowed from humans. Blue is my favourite colour. If all else fails, my song and dance routine might do the trick!

21

··· Lotus flower ···
SPOTLESSLY CLEAN

I am a flower beetle and let me tell you about my favourite thing in the world: the lotus flower. This awesome flower rises high above muddy water to unfold its large petals in the warm sunshine. As it blooms, it releases heat and an exquisite perfume to entice little critters like me who are looking for food. When night falls and the flower closes up, I linger around for a warm shelter and a pollen feast. The next morning I am off, moving the pollen to another lotus flower to produce seeds and new plants.

Despite growing in muddy lakes and ponds, this sweet flower keeps itself spotlessly clean. How does it do it? Although its leaves look smooth, they are actually covered in thousands of tiny, waxy bumps. Droplets of water collect on the bumps and, with the slightest breeze, roll off and take dirt particles with them. Nothing sticks!

ArtScience Museum, Singapore

The beauty of the lotus flower has also inspired some very cool buildings in the human world, from a museum in Singapore to a temple in India.

This striking flower shelters bugs like me, and now its design shelters humans too!

Having solved the self-cleaning mystery of the lotus flower, humans are copying the clever texture of its leaves for all kinds of outdoor things that need to stay clean, from paint to glass, tiles, fabrics and more. A good clean with just rainwater has to be a great idea and the lotus flower worked it out millions of years ago!

STAYING CLEAN

YOGA for BEETLES

Flower Power

LOTUS EFFECT PAINT

··· Blue mussel ···
SUPERGLUE

The life of a mussel is like the tide – it has its highs and lows! We mussels are happy to clump together on the seashore, clinging to rocks to avoid being washed away by the waves. But when uncovered at low tide, we become a buffet for hungry seabirds. And, of course, there is always the risk of ending up on a plate of seafood linguine.

GLUE

Each one of us builds a sturdy home to protect its soft body, using minerals from the sea. It's made of two shells that can close with a bit of mussel power when there is danger or too little water around.

To anchor ourselves to wet rocks, we squirt a kind of liquid glue that hardens quickly in water, forming fine, sticky threads called byssus. These look a bit like scratchy beard hairs but they are actually as strong as bungee cords.

WATER IN

WATER OUT

SHELL

BYSSUS

FOOT

ECO GLUE

Mussel Muscles

MUSSEL GLUE

STICKING TOGETHER
HANGING ON

Moules marinières

GOING
with the
FLOW

Inspired by our biological brilliance, humans have mimicked our sticky threads to create an eco-friendly glue. 'Mussel glue' is strong, waterproof and is not harmful to wildlife. **Imagine all the things it could be used for, like repairing ships, pipelines and cool, futuristic underwater buildings.**

... Diabolical ironclad beetle ...
UNCRUSHABLE ARMOUR

I am probably the toughest critter on the planet, hence my name: the diabolical ironclad beetle. My home is the west coast of the United States, where you can find me under a rock or the bark of a tree. I can't fly but I do have super-tough armour that can resist the pecks and nips of hungry birds, lizards and rodents. Nothing can crush me, not even a car!

THE SECRET OF MY SUPER-TOUGH DESIGN

I'm built like a tiny tank on six legs: my shell is flat, lies low to the ground and can take enormous pressure without breaking. While other beetles gracefully open their wing cases to fly, mine are locked together like the pieces of a jigsaw puzzle, forming an indestructible shield.

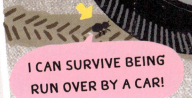

I CAN SURVIVE BEING RUN OVER BY A CAR!

Diabolically Tough

Uncrushable Materials

IRONCLAD

Now that humans have cracked the secret of my uncrackable shell, they are looking at how to mimic its structure to make their buildings, planes and other constructions even stronger and tougher.

Having been around for millions of years, we've had plenty of time to develop our super-strong shell.

Never underestimate the power of a small beetle!

··· Mantis shrimp ···
SMASHING CLAWS

I am a small crustacean, and you can find me burrowed into the sand around a coral reef. Don't let my beautiful colours dazzle you! I am the very definition of small but mighty – I throw the fastest punch on Earth.

My front claws are like two big spring-loaded clubs. I can whip them out faster than the blink of an eye to smash open the shells of tasty crabs or deter anything that wants to eat me. What's my secret? My claws are made of different materials layered in intricate patterns, which make them incredibly strong and impact-resistant.

Humans are baffled that a tiny creature like me can repeatedly deliver such a powerful punch without breaking. They are hoping to mimic the structure of my club-like claws to create new materials for things that need to be tough and shock-resistant like helmets, robots, aeroplanes, wind turbines and more.

It's no wonder they call me the SMASHER!

World Records

MUHAMMAD ALI

MANTIS

SHRIMP

WORLD RECORD
THE MOST POWERFUL PUNCH IN THE ANIMAL KINGDOM

··· Darwin's bark spider ···
EXCEPTIONAL SILK

I am a small, inconspicuous spider with a spinning talent. I build the world's largest webs with silk. But my silk is not ordinary – it's the toughest natural material on the planet. My home is the deep jungle of Madagascar, where I spin gigantic sticky webs over rivers and streams to catch flying insects for my dinner.

I was born to spin! With my spinnerets, I produce different kinds of silk for different uses. To make my web, I spray a long thread of silk into the breeze until it latches onto a twig or leaf on the other side of the river. Once the first line is anchored, I walk along it like a tightrope and start spinning a beautiful spirally web.

WEB CONSTRUCTION

STRUCTURAL SILK

CATCHING SILK

REINFORCED JOINING POINTS

ANATOMY

LEG
PALP
EYES
ABDOMEN
SPINNERETS

THIS IS THE LENGTH OF MY WEB!

Humans have known about the exceptional qualities of spider silk for thousands of years. It's as strong as steel, but as stretchy as rubber. It's lightweight but incredibly tough. Untangling our secret is helping them to develop new materials that are light, but super strong.

One day, bridges and buildings might be held up by artificial spider silk rather than steel – but they won't be catching any bugs like I do!

··· *Abalone* ···

ONE TOUGH SHELL

I am a simple seaweed-eating sea snail. I have a large frilly foot that looks nothing like your feet but does allow me to hang on to rocks. Like many marine creatures, I build a shell to protect myself from predators, using simple materials from seawater. But MINE is the toughest of all!

Under the dull exterior of my shell is hidden a colourful shiny interior. This inner layer is not only beautiful but also super tough. The secret is how it is built – like layers of tiny bricks on top of each other and held together with stretchy glue. This allows the bricks to slide under impact without breaking.

Humans have coveted pearly shells like mine for centuries to make jewellery, buttons and musical instruments. They are now intrigued by the way I build my tough, lightweight and durable home, as it could inspire new ultra-strong materials that can be assembled without heat or mighty machines.

Marine Home Show

Venus comb

Queen conch

So, the next time you see pretty shells on the beach, think of all the ingenious building work that went into making them. **The sea is filled with amazing constructions. Who knows what else these could inspire!**

Chambered nautilus

Eyed Cowrie

33

···Venus' flower basket sponge···
HOUSE OF GLASS

Despite my name, I am neither a flower nor a basket! I am a simple animal living a simple life in the darkness of the deep sea. I don't have a mouth, brain, heart or muscles! Unlike most animals, I am attached to the seabed and can't swim or crawl. So I build a long tube-like skeleton that allows me to pump water in and filter all the food I need.

SPICULE

My skeleton can withstand strong currents and the odd bump from other sea creatures and yet it is made of glass. What's my secret? From seawater I create teeny, spiky bits of glass, called spicules, which I build into a very strong structure.

Like most sea sponges of my kind, I have a pair of lifelong lodgers – two small shrimps who moved in as larvae and have grown too large to leave! They clean my basket and, in return, they get food and a safe home.

WATER OUT

WATER IN

'THE GHERKIN' UNITED KINGDOM

This building may look like a pickled cucumber but, in fact, it was inspired by me! Its rounded shape and criss-cross pattern mimic my skeleton. Its structure is extra strong and designed to draw fresh air into the entire building. **What I do so well underwater, this building does in the air.**

35

··· Earthworm ···
SOIL BUILDER

I am a humble wriggly worm.
I like to keep out of sight, but I'm
always hard at work under your feet.
As an animal builder, my job is to
turn dead plants into rich soil for new
plants to grow, including the ones you eat.
I share my patch of earth with billions
of other soil makers, from fungi to
tiny creepy-crawlies.

SOIL BUILDER

MITE

SPRINGTAIL

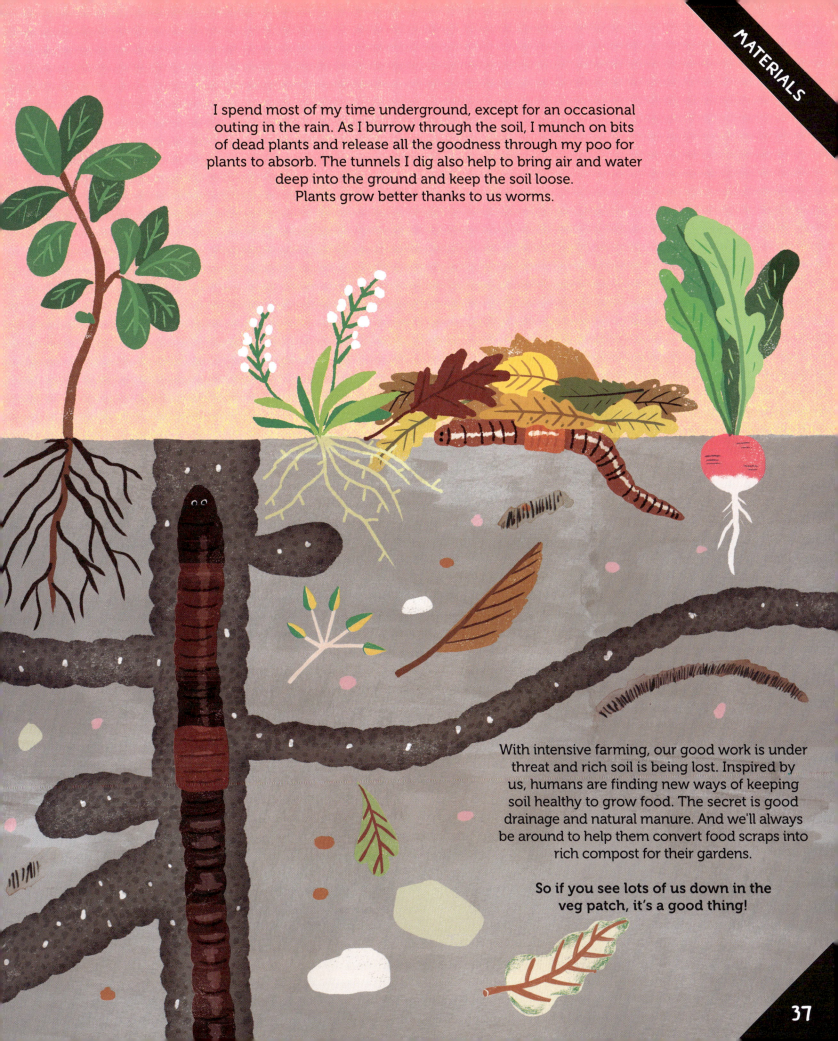

I spend most of my time underground, except for an occasional outing in the rain. As I burrow through the soil, I munch on bits of dead plants and release all the goodness through my poo for plants to absorb. The tunnels I dig also help to bring air and water deep into the ground and keep the soil loose.
Plants grow better thanks to us worms.

With intensive farming, our good work is under threat and rich soil is being lost. Inspired by us, humans are finding new ways of keeping soil healthy to grow food. The secret is good drainage and natural manure. And we'll always be around to help them convert food scraps into rich compost for their gardens.

So if you see lots of us down in the veg patch, it's a good thing!

BUILDING MATERIALS

Welcome to our library of building materials! As animal builders, we use the best stuff for the job. It all depends on design. Twigs, leaves and pebbles help to create strong structures. Materials that are workable like mud or stretchy like cobwebs are ideal for shaping nests. Feathers and moss make a soft, warm interior. All the materials we use are totally natural – except for a few bits and bobs left behind by humans.

FROM PLANTS

Made of plants, spider silk and lichen

LOGS & STICKS

MOSS

LICHEN

Grass & Leaves

FLOWERS

FROM ANIMALS

COBWEBS

SHELLS

FUR

DUNG

Feathers

FROM MINERALS

PEBBLES & STONES

Made of mud

FROM HUMANS *NOT Recommended*

THESE DONT BREAK DOWN NATURALLY!

··· Durian fruit ···
SPIKY SUN SHADES

The durian fruit might be smelly and prickly but it has to be admired for its clever shape. The formidable spikes keep birds and small creatures at bay until the fruit ripens and protect it when it falls to the ground. They also stop the hidden seeds from overheating in the tropical sun.

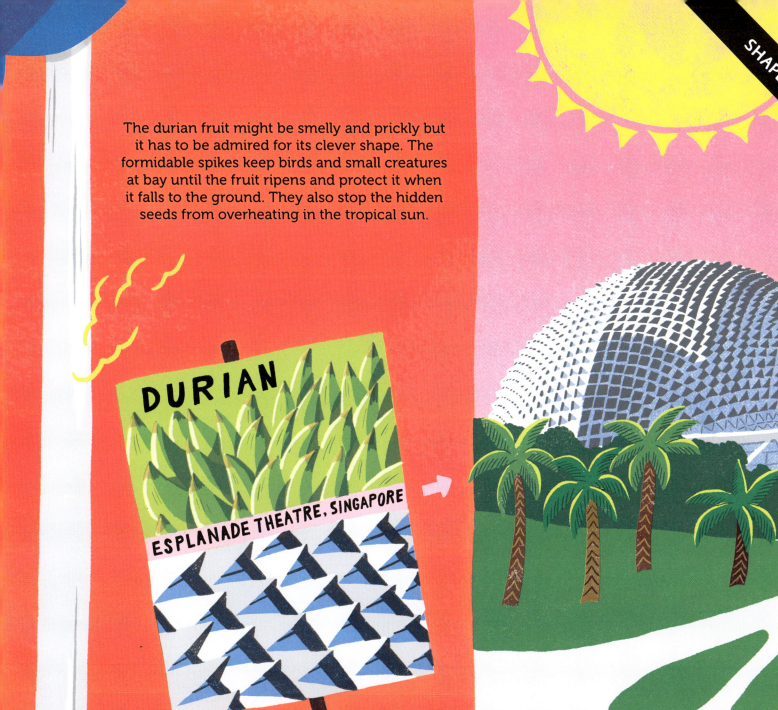

This cool building could easily be mistaken for a humongous durian! Just like my favourite fruit, it is covered in spikes to provide shade from the sun. Special shutters adjust to the angle of the sun to keep the heat out and let the light in.

When it comes to the durian fruit, you either like it or hate it. I LOVE it and it seems that human architects do too.

... *White-spotted puffer fish* ...
ART IN THE SAND

I am a timid kind of fish and I live in warm, shallow waters in the Pacific Ocean. I don't have the bright colours or bold stripes of other tropical fish and my swimming is a bit clumsy. I tend to blend in and I'm almost invisible. But I have a secret artistic talent and I never shy away from hard work.

W. S. Pufferfish

I create this grand piece of art at the bottom of the sea, using only two small fins as my tools. Day and night I plough the sand to break it up into fine particles. Flapping my fins, I dig grooves and build ridges into intricate patterns. Then I add the finishing touch – a few seashells for decoration. Why do I go to all this trouble? To find the best mate and to make the best nest!

I AM HERE

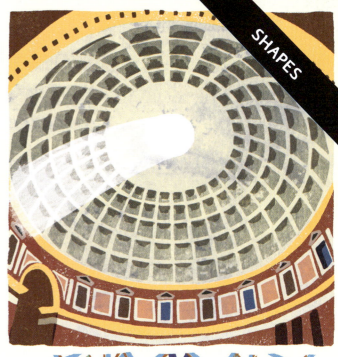

My creation has perfect symmetry, as one side mirrors the other. I can do all this without a ruler or a compass. Humans have always marvelled at and copied the symmetrical shapes found in nature. **I hope my labour of love inspires even more beautiful patterns in the human world.**

··· Desert snail ···
COOL MOBILE HOME

Slowly, slowly, slowly, I crawl along the ground leaving a slimy trail behind me. I am a simple creature really. I have one long muscular foot to push me forwards and two eyes on long stalks so I can look up, down and all around. Most of my distant relatives can be found in damp, dark places, hiding under rocks and rotten logs to stay moist. But I live in the hot, barren desert with hardly any water at all. How do I do it?

HOME IS WHERE MY SHELL IS ♥

Like all snails, I carry my home around on my back and, as I grow, it grows too. My shell is perfectly suited for a life in the scorching sun where there are very few places to hide. It's chalky white and curved to reflect the sun and has a very small entrance to keep the heat out. It's also hard and thick to protect me from predators.

To avoid drying up in hot weather, I do spend most of my time tucked deep into my spirally home where it is cooler. I only come out a few days during the rainy season to look for food and can quickly zip back into my shell at the first sign of a hungry gerbil! In my cosy home, I can survive droughts for years without food or water.

MILKY WAY

CAR PARK

HORN

Spiral staircase

CURVY DESERT HOME

HURRICANE

SPIRAL SHAPES

Seashell

Human builders have been inspired by spirals found in nature for centuries. Now my shell, with its unique shape and colour, is the inspiration for a new desert dwelling that stays cool without air conditioning. The white curvy roof reflects sunlight and humans can escape the heat by going deep into their home, as I do.

After all, we've managed to survive in the desert for millions of years and know a thing or two about keeping cool!

··· Peacock ···
LIGHT TRICKS

I am a spectacular bird who likes to show off to impress a mate. Blending in isn't an option for me anyway – not with such long tail feathers bursting with colour! To flaunt my beautiful 'eye' spots, I open my feathers like a fan and shake them. Like magic, they change colour in the light.

Most animals and plants get their colours from 'pigments'. These absorb all the colours that make up light, except the one you see, which is reflected back to your eye. But I have another trick up my feathers. Tiny ridges on their surface scatter light to produce brilliant yellows, greens and blues. When I strut about, the shape of these ridges make my tail colours appear to change.

BIRDS of a FEATHER

Flamboyant Feathers

TALES of TAILS

THE PROUD PEACOCK

My flamboyant plumage has always captivated humans. Mastering my clever tricks could help them to make paint or building materials that use light to create colours, like my feathers. Or it could lead to brighter, more colourful screens for smartphones and computers that use much less power.

My naturally brilliant colours will continue to turn heads!

SUPER NEST BUILDERS

How do you build a home using no more than a beak, claws, plants and twigs? Birds certainly win the award for ingenuity in design! Meet some of our master builders who can turn local materials into architectural gems, without a speck of waste!

Tailorbirds
METICULOUS NEEDLEWORK

We use our long beaks as needles to pierce a series of holes along the edges of a leaf. We then stitch the edges together with a thread of spider silk or plant fibre. Inside the leaf, we weave a cup of grass and line it with soft feathers and fur to keep our chicks warm and cosy. And the fresh, green leaves provide perfect camouflage!

Ovenbirds
MASTER SCULPTORS

After rain, we gather pellets of mud and mix them with bits of plants to shape into a neat dome, leaving a small entrance on the side. Inside, we build a chamber with a dividing wall to keep our chicks safe. The tropical sun finishes the job by baking our nest rock hard.

CHAMBER

Weaver birds
A HANGING HOME

To construct our suspended home, we cut long blades of grass and leaves with our short, blunt beaks. We then carefully weave these together to make our hanging nest, preferably from a branch over water for extra protection. The finishing touch is a long tube-shaped entrance and a comfy interior of grass and feathers. We often build our nests close together, as we like to chatter and twitter.

Humans
BEIJING NATIONAL STADIUM, CHINA

This giant nest of twisted steel, woven around a massive bowl, was obviously not built by our feathered friends – but it does hint at their designs. Made to hold the Olympic Games, it is a strong building that provides a magnificent space for the humans inside. It can even resist earthquakes!

2008 SUMMER OLYMPICS

49

··· Oriental hornet ···
SOLAR POWERED

Like bees, we have a busy life, buzzing around in our large colony under the command of our queen. We live in hot, sunny places so we dig cool underground nests. With our spit we turn bits of soil into a hard material to build perfect hexagon-shaped cells for our young.

Unlike bees, we work harder when the sun is at its brightest and it's scorching hot. This is because we are solar-powered marvels! Our bright yellow and brown stripes contain special substances that trap and absorb the sun's light and turn it into electricity. It gives us an extra jolt of energy for all our digging and flying around.

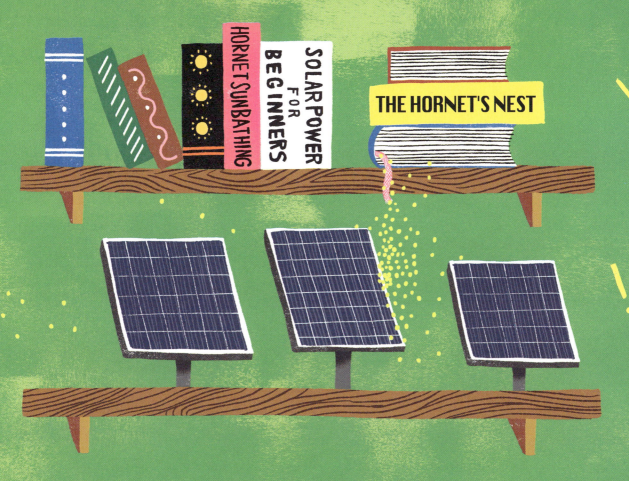

We've had millions of years to perfect our solar cells, so we are way ahead of humans when it comes to solar energy! With our help, they hope to find more efficient ways of collecting energy from the sun to power their homes, buildings and machines.

In the future, we might be more famous for our solar power than for our stinging power!

... Firefly ...
GLOWING LANTERN

I am a firefly but I am not a fly.
In fact, I am a small winged beetle with magical powers. I glow in the dark! When night falls, I use my special lantern to impress a mate or warn predators to stay away. Creating my own light is very useful, as I am a night-loving insect who likes to shine beneath the stars.

How do I produce this magical glow? Let me shed a little light: it's all to do with chemistry. Each flicker of light is sparked by a chemical reaction that takes place inside my body. It creates the best lighting on the planet! When these chemicals combine, the light I produce gives very little heat, making me the most energy-efficient light bulb ever.

Taking a closer look under a microscope, humans have worked out that my glow is made extra bright by the shape of my lantern. Its surface is covered in tiny jagged scales that stick out at different angles. These scatter the light and help me to shine even more.

No wonder my impressive light show has given humans a bright idea! Copying my lantern could make their light bulbs more efficient and help to save energy too.

So next time you spot a firefly, keep in mind that our flickering is not just a wonder of the night. It might be the key to a brighter world!

... *Prairie dog* ...
FRESH BURROW

Humans call me a prairie dog but I look nothing like a dog. **It must be because I bark loudly when there is danger.** I'm a cute, chubby rodent who scurries in and out of holes in the open prairies of North America. And I'm very sociable too! I live with thousands of others, in a large group called a town, and we all greet each other with a kiss.

NURSERY

Our sharp claws make us expert diggers and we use these to create our famous burrows. When not busy foraging for grass, roots and seeds, we dig and re-dig. Our underground burrows can be super large, with many entrances and tunnels. We also have separate rooms for nurseries, sleeping, listening posts and even bathrooms.

And that's not even the half of it.
We have a cool solution to keep the air fresh in our long burrows. It's simple. We build two entrances, one higher than the other. Because air moves faster higher up, the higher entrance sucks out stale air while fresh air is drawn into the lower entrance, creating a nice breeze through the burrow. And the earth mound we make for the higher entrance is also a great lookout for spotting hungry badgers, coyotes or eagles.

Humans use giant machines in their buildings to bring in fresh air and pump stale air out. Our natural air-con system could change the way they cool and refresh the air in their dwellings without using energy.

It's just a question of knowing how to use the wind.

BEDROOM

BATHROOM

55

··· Termite ···
AIR–CON TOWER

I share a home with millions of friends and life in here is all hustle and bustle. As a worker termite, my jobs are endless. When I'm not building or repairing the nest, I collect food, wait on our queen, carry her eggs to the nurseries and raise her young. I also tend to the fungus garden, which provides our main source of food. Meanwhile, soldier termites, armed with their menacing mandibles, work hard at guarding the colony against raiding armies of deadly ants.

CENTRAL CHIMNEY

FUNGUS GARDEN

GROUND ENTRANCE

ROYAL CELL

NURSERY

We worker termites may be as small as a grain of rice but we know how to build big. With just blobs of soil, spit and dung, we construct skyscrapers – at least, by termite standards! Living in the hot savannah calls for ingenuity, so we create our own air-con system. We build a network of tunnels, chimneys and vents to draw cool, fresh air into our nest below and allow hot, stale air to escape.

EASTGATE CENTRE ZIMBABWE

OUR QUEEN

BUILDING WITH SPIT AND POO

LIFE UNDERGROUND

FUNGUS GARDEN

Keeping Cool

Inspired by our towering homes, humans are now constructing buildings that can cool themselves in hot climates. Just like our mounds, they have ducts, chimneys and walls that allow air to pass through and keep their residents cool and fresh. And this saves a lot of energy too.

When it comes to natural air con, humans did well to take a leaf out of our building manual.

··· Toucan ···
COOL BILL

My home is the hot, steamy jungle of **South America and my best feature is my big, beautiful bill.** Not only does it make me look handsome, but it's also the perfect tool for plucking fruit from the tips of tree branches. My bill might seem heavy and cumbersome but it is surprisingly light and strong. Its surface is made of the same material as your fingernails and the inside is like a honeycomb full of air pockets.

RAINFOREST SURVIVAL

WONDERFUL BEAKS

Air-con Engineer

SOUTH AMERICA

When it comes to keeping cool in the hot tropics, my giant beak fits the bill! It is laced with blood vessels and has no feathers to keep the heat in. When it's hot, I push more blood into my bill to let heat escape into the air and stay cool. When it's cold at night, I reduce the blood flow to conserve heat and stay warm.

BE PROUD OF YOUR BEAK

LIGHT & STRONG

SHOCK ABSORBENT

HELPS TO STAY COOL

KERATIN (LIKE FINGERNAILS)

HONEYCOMB

My giant bill is inspiring new materials that need to be light and strong. Its special design can also help humans to find new ways of keeping their homes cool without using energy. Imagine walls and roofs that can let heat escape into the air when needed, just like my beak.

Toucan bill air con could be the next big thing in cooling buildings!

··· Tree ···
POWER PLANT

This ancient oak tree was planted by one of my ancestors. Over hundreds of years, it has grown from a small acorn, hidden away as food for the winter, to a magnificent old tree. Many creatures, including myself, come here to look for food and make their homes. It's a very busy building site indeed!

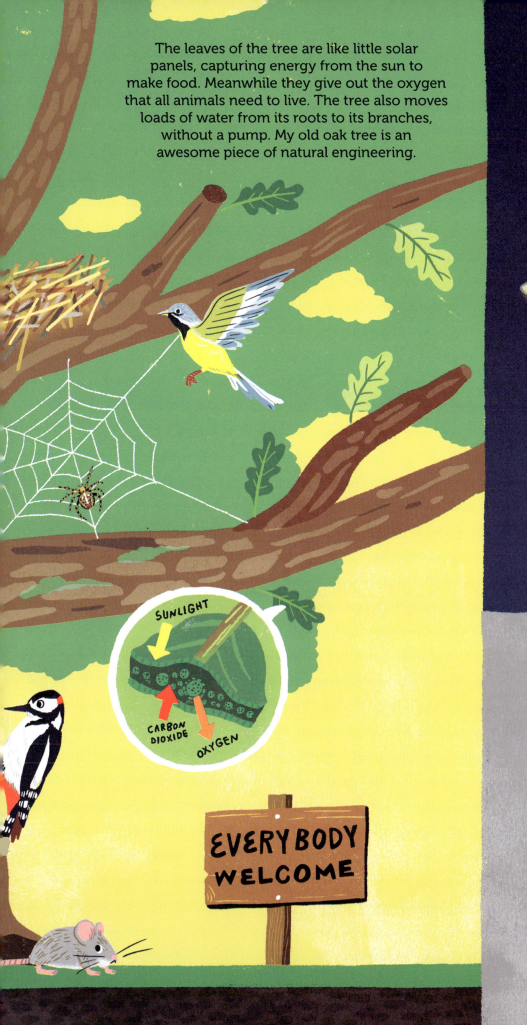

The leaves of the tree are like little solar panels, capturing energy from the sun to make food. Meanwhile they give out the oxygen that all animals need to live. The tree also moves loads of water from its roots to its branches, without a pump. My old oak tree is an awesome piece of natural engineering.

SUNLIGHT

CARBON DIOXIDE

OXYGEN

EVERYBODY WELCOME

Humans know that burning coal, oil and gas to produce energy is not good for the planet. Inspired by trees like mine, they are finding better ways of capturing and storing the sun's energy to light up their homes and cities.

This cool street lamp with its long green trunk and leaf-like solar panels can harness the sun's energy to produce electricity. **It looks like a tree, and works like one too!**

KEEPING COOL

To stay cool, some animals build their own air-conditioned homes while others look for a shady spot or just spray themselves with water. Find out how some of us have other unusual ways to cool off.

Black-tailed jackrabbit
AIR–CON EARS

Thanks to my very long ears, I manage to stay cool in the hot American desert where I live. My ears are packed with blood vessels and they work like mini air conditioners. When it gets too hot, more blood flows into my ears to let heat escape and cool me down. Of course, large ears are also useful when listening for danger.

Saharan silver ant
WALKING MIRROR

I live in the blistering hot Sahara desert and my strategy to stay cool is one of the coolest. The top and sides of my body are covered in special silvery hairs that reflect and scatter sunlight. Not only do they shield me from the sun's heat, but they also give me a rather cool metallic glint.

Purple sea star
WATER PUMP

Living on a rocky shore between high and low tides has its challenges. When the tide goes out and I am busy munching mussels, I am often left exposed to the sun. I have a unique technique to stop overheating. When submerged at high tide, I soak up plenty of cold seawater and this helps to keep my whole body cool when the tide recedes.

Cape ground squirrel
BUILT–IN PARASOL

Parasols are not a new invention. Desert ground squirrels like me have been using them for millions of years. How? By using our tails of course! I can use my long, bushy tail to shield myself from the hot sun of southern Africa. When the heat gets unbearable, I can always retreat into my cool burrow.

No wonder humans are turning to us for the coolest cooling solutions. With our help, they might one day find better ways of cooling their buildings and machines, without using too much energy.

··· Camel ···
WATER–SAVING NOSE

Imagine a place with huge sandy dunes, very little water and a hot, scorching sun all year round. This is my home: the desert. Fortunately, life here suits me very well. My coarse hair protects me from the sun and my hump stores fat for when food is scarce. I have been complimented for my long eyelashes, but they don't just look good; they also protect my eyes from the sand.

My ancestors have been ferrying humans and heavy loads across the desert for thousands of years. We have always been admired for our extraordinary ability to go without water for weeks. Recently, humans have discovered how we do this. It's all down to our cleverly designed nose!

MOIST SURFACE

HOT AIR

COOL AIR

COOL SURFACE

CONDENSED WATER

Not only can I close my nostrils to keep the sand out but my nose also helps me to retain precious water. All animals, even you, release a little bit of water in the form of vapour when they breathe out. Thanks to the special lining of my nose, I can capture this moisture from my breath and return it to my body. As I breathe out, the air begins to cool and condenses into water along my nose.

DESERT GARDENING

GREENHOUSE

Having discovered my nasal tricks, humans are hoping to mimic the way I pull moisture from the air to make the desert bloom. This could help with all kinds of things in places where there is very little rain, from growing food in greenhouses to storing drinking water. **My nose has become more famous than my hump.**

··· Thorny devil ···
WATER PUMP

Despite my prickly appearance, I am totally harmless, unless you happen to be an ant! I can eat thousands of them in a single meal. My home is the arid desert of Australia where I live a solitary life. As you can see, I am covered from head to tail with spines and this makes me a rather unappealing snack, except for a few desperate birds and snakes.

I drink water in the most unusual way – with my skin! As it hardly ever rains here, I need every drop I can get. I am covered in small grooves that run between my spines and lead to the corners of my mouth. To drink, I flick sand dampened by the morning dew onto my skin and draw moisture out of it into my grooves, like a sponge.

AUSTRALIA

YOU ARE HERE ✗

THORNY DEVIL'S TERRITORY

Humans are studying how I can make water travel all the way up to my mouth without a pump or using energy. My unique drinking habits may just hold the key to finding better ways of pumping water to the top of tall buildings or harvesting water where there is very little rain.

A thorny devil's solution to a thorny challenge!

··· Wetland ···
WATER FILTER

I am a shy little water vole who likes to move between land and water. To make this semi-aquatic life easy, I dig my burrow in a grassy riverbank, with many entrances above and below the water. I have plenty of plants to nibble on and lots of fast escape routes if needed. At the sight of a mighty mink, I can quickly retreat into my burrow.

DIRTY WATER

CLEAN WATER

RATTY & FRIENDS

But let me tell you about the brilliant plants that grow in the watery wetland that is my home. Not only are these plants my favourite food, but they also act as a water filter. Their dense leaves and tangled roots help to slow down water flowing from the land into the river and clean it by trapping waste.

PROTECT OUR WETLANDS

WIND in the WILLOWS

Humans are taking a leaf out of nature's book to clean up their act. Many of the things they do to grow food on farms or make stuff in factories pollute rivers and lakes. They are now starting to build artificial wetlands like the one where I live to clean their water. **This is good news for all of us and for our rivers too!**

ECO—FRIENDLY PACKAGING

Plants make amazing packaging to preserve their seeds and fruit. Think of pinecones, acorns and banana skins. But some animals are also experts at creating the perfect packaging to protect their young. Meet some of the very best in the business!

MALLARD

CARRION CROW

STARLING

HOUSE SPARROW

BEE HUMMINGBIRD

PHEASANT

OSTRICH

EMU

GUILLEMOT

OSPREY

WORLD'S LARGEST EGGS

Ostrich
EGG PACKAGING

We birds lay eggs with a hard shell to protect our chicks before they hatch. Eggs can hold a good supply of food and water, and allow air in and out for our growing chicks to breathe. Despite being the world's heaviest bird, even I can sit happily on my eggs without them breaking. That's smart packaging!

Emperor moth
SILKY COCOON

Moths like me start life as a teeny egg and grow rapidly into a hungry, hairy caterpillar. When the time comes to transform into a beautiful moth, we find a good hiding spot amongst plants and spin a strong cocoon made of coarse brown silk. When ready to emerge, the cocoon simply splits open and we take to the air.

Foam-nest tree frog
BUBBLE WRAP

I am a small tree frog with a knack for bubble wrap! To make my nest, I choose a branch over the water and produce a gooey liquid, which I whip into a bubbly foam with my back legs. I lay my eggs inside the foam and let the sun dry the outside into a hard crust. When my tadpoles hatch, they wriggle out and drop into the water below. Plop! Plop! Plop!

Unlike most packaging created by humans, all our eggs, cocoons and bubbles disappear or break down over time so there is no waste. The good news is that humans are following our lead to find new forms of packaging that could do the same.

ANIMAL BUILDING SCHOOL

Welcome to our building school where we share our best tricks and strategies to help human builders find solutions to tricky problems. There is so much to discover in the world of animal builders and we hope to spark lots of new ideas!

- ☑ CUBE–SHAPED
- ☑ DOESN'T ROLL AWAY
- ☑ CAN BE STACKED
- ☑ NOT SMELLY!

Wombat
SQUARE POO

I am a furry little animal native to Australia, with amazing digging skills and a very peculiar habit – I produce square poo! I leave square droppings as a calling card to mark my territory and they can't roll away. Could the unusual design of my gut inspire humans to make their own cube-shaped objects without having to mould or cut them into the right shape?

Pangolin
ARMOUR—PLATED PROTECTION

I am a rather shy, slow-moving mammal but I am equipped with the best coat of armour. I am covered from head to claw in hard overlapping scales and, when there is danger, I roll into a tight ball to protect myself. Could my unique coat of armour inspire new kinds of roofs with flexible, protective scales like mine?

Star-nosed mole
SUPER—SENSORY NOSE

I am a small mole with two shovel-like front paws and a star for a nose. I spend most of my time underground in complete darkness and my unusual nose helps me to feel the world around me. Could I inspire clever machines that can feel their way in the dark?

On your next nature walk, look carefully at all the animals and plants around you.
The next coolest building idea might be lurking under a rock or hiding high up in a tree!

AWARD CEREMONY

All animal builders featured in this book have outstanding skills and talents, from digging and weaving to lighting and interior design. Can you match the winners with their awards?

Darwin's bark spider

Tailorbird

Bee, Ant and Termite

Prairie dog

Firefly

Earthworm

Puffer fish

Bowerbird

Beaver

Weaver bird

Ironclad Beetle

Peacock

BEST DIGGER AWARD

BEST
Recycling
AWARD

BEST
STITCHING

BEST
TEAM
WORK

BEST WEAVING

BEST
PROTECTIVE
GEAR
AWARD
1

BEST
COLOURS
AWARD

BEST
DAM
ENGINEER

BEST
LIGHTING

BEST
DECORATOR

BEST
ARTIST

BEST
SPINNING

SEE ANSWERS ON PAGE 77

INDEX

AWARD CEREMONY ANSWERS

Best spinning award: Darwin's bark spider
Best artist award: Puffer fish
Best decorator award: Bowerbird
Best protective gear award: Ironclad beetle
Best lighting award: Firefly
Best dam engineer award: Beaver
Best colours award: Peacock
Best weaving award: Weaver bird
Best teamwork award: Bee, ant and termite
Best stitching award: Tailorbird
Best recycling award: Earthworm
Best digger award: Prairie dog

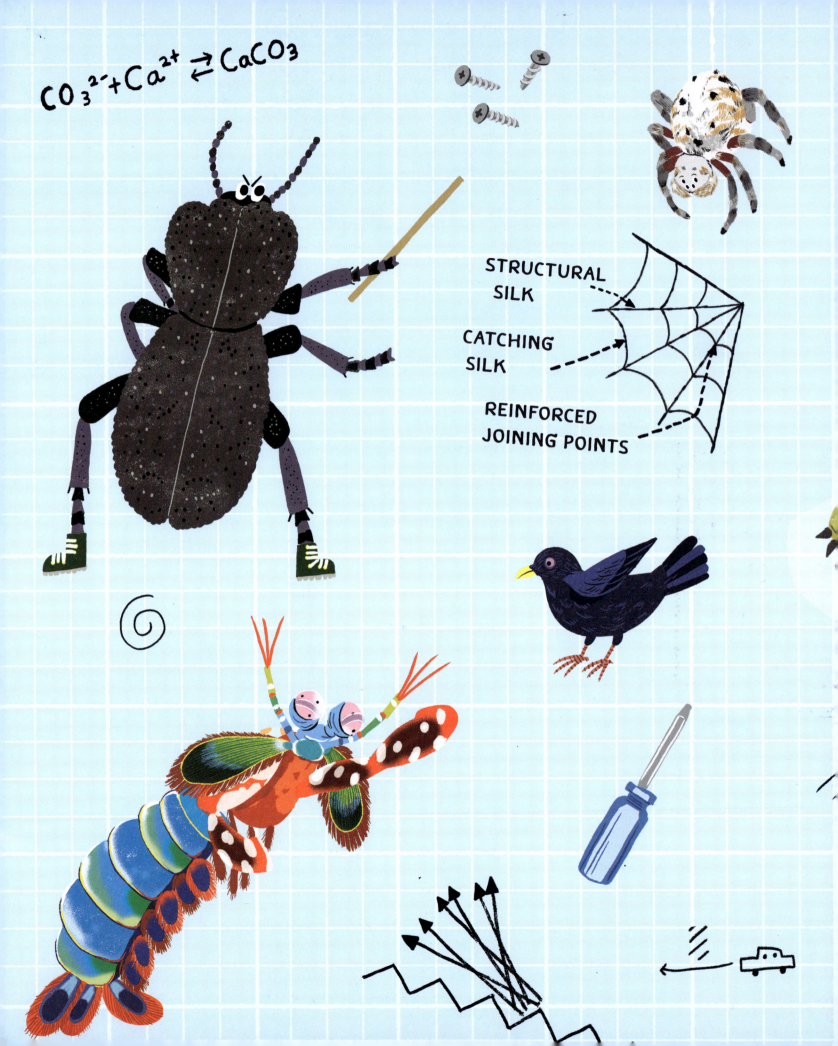

$$CO_3^{2-} + Ca^{2+} \rightleftharpoons CaCO_3$$

STRUCTURAL
SILK

CATCHING
SILK

REINFORCED
JOINING POINTS